FANCY CLAPPING

FANCY CLAPPING

MARK D. DUNN

ScrivenerPress

Library and Archives Canada Cataloguing in Publication

Dunn, Mark D., 1969-
    Fancy Clapping / Mark D. Dunn.

Poems
ISBN 978-1-896350-48-6

    I. Title.

PS8557.U548517F35   2012   C811'.6   C2012-900544-4

Book design: Laurence Steven
Cover design: Chris Evans
Cover illustration: Gary Barwin
Photo of author: Maria Parrella-Ilaria

Published by Scrivener Press
465 Loach's Road,
Sudbury, Ontario, Canada, P3E 2R2
info@yourscrivenerpress.com
www.scrivenerpress.com

We acknowledge the financial support of the Ontario Arts Council, the Canada Council for the Arts, and the Government of Canada through the Canada Book Fund for our publishing activities.

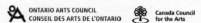

ONTARIO ARTS COUNCIL
CONSEIL DES ARTS DE L'ONTARIO

Canada Council   Conseil des Arts
for the Arts   du Canada

Canadian   Patrimoine
Heritage   canadien

for Maria

Knowing that everything comes to an end is a gift of experience, a consolation gift for knowing that we ourselves are coming to an end. Before we get it we live in a continuous present, and imagine the future as more of that present. Happiness is endless happiness. Pain is endless pain.
—Tobias Wolff, *This Boy's Life*

How can there be laughter, how can there be pleasure, when the whole world is burning? When you are in deep darkness, will you not ask for a lamp?
—*The Dhammapada*, 11.1

Let's dance.
—David Bowie

CONTENTS

I

II

III

IV

A SHORT ROUND

I

Maps to the Underworld (1)

There is no mercy for the poet who enters uninvited.
The gates crashed, and no party within.
Stumbling, bound in a darkness
that is fearless of the sun, batting cobwebs,
he moves along rock walls
guided by the daylight fading behind him.

Yet drawn in, welcomed to the cave,
he leaves with a prize, some power over flesh.

Or oblivious, waking from a nap under a tree,
not knowing that the ground is no longer ground,
that the trees are no longer in dialogue with his lungs,
sun no longer the sun, but the memory of these things,
he stays for a year and a day,
returns without losing a moment.

o

Forcing the veil aside, he shrugs away grace.
A willed transilience that offends
all who've earned their deaths.

I Can Drive if You Like

i

It is strange at night
how the road ends
and a day of travel still ahead.

Part of this poem
had me run a red light
on a Michigan highway.

No one was coming
but I didn't know that.
There was no other way
for me at the moment

but to run the red light
while pacing this poem,
turn into the gas station
and leave the engine on.

I'm writing it down
at the counter,
paying for the gas.

The guy stares
like he hears ghost music
from across a lake.

M in the bathroom
thanking the gods.

The red light low
like a firefly on the windshield.

And so far she hasn't said a word about it,
no hint of iron between us.

She'd said
      Red Light.
          Red Light.
              Red Light.

With me braking softly but late
and no cars coming, so I turned…
M in the seat, breathing.
Sorry, I said. Perhaps
our hands touched.

ii

It is strange at night, twenty years on
and still strange. I remember the song
that played when the Mazda with bad brakes
took out my grandfather's minivan.

The glass froth, pellets
from the side window,
stinging—it may have been
hail, or tacks from the carpeted sky
popping away.

In the blind spin, the whole
earth became a blur of snow,
a one-eighty twist on ice.

The Mazda would have made it
across the country without stopping
had I not taken my green light.

No one shouts
                    Green Light.
Just a nod, a nudge, a glance to the sky.

The forgotten Beatle on the radio.
Nothing came easy for him,
or for me at that moment.

I stepped out to the intersection
and left the van running in gear,
coughing forward, a wounded train.

The man in the Mazda making his escape
leaked brown fluid from a flattened nose,
parts of my body in his grille.

Where are the spirits
now that I'm driving?

Ghosts in the fog
along the highway
are stuck to their places.

In this car, I am quicker than the dead.

Modern Religion in New York City

i

The statue of Atlas
across the street from a cathedral
gathers tourists at his feet,
their cameras flashing. He is
holding the world after all,
while the brick church does nothing
but keep rain off its pews;
its doors locked to the homeless.

ii

She is from Kansas or California,
France maybe, wears a t-shirt with John Lennon
in a t-shirt, a silver peace medallion,
a crow's foot, on a chain from her neck,
and takes a photo of her husband
where Lennon stood and fell.

iii

Through the walls, a voice,
"God. Oh, God. Yes. God. Yes."
As the ice in the bucket on the rattling fridge
settles with the sound of a crystal wine glass
rolling on the deck of a listing ship.
Tomorrow is Sunday. I have no plans.

Boys

Back in the day when bodies were mysterious
we marvelled at the pencil sketches of lovers
from a book stashed in our parents' closets,
and watched out the window,
all night if we had to,
until the girl across the street
changed her sweater.

No class teaches how to speak
with the girl you've spied on.
In the cafeteria or library she takes
the seat beside you. A few years older,
confident, she is not worried
what anyone might think. She just
sits there, waiting you think,
to be spoken to. And what to say?

There is no incantation to humanize the image.
It is the death of a double life,
or the beginning.
Could you one day, after the altar,
on a Lake Tahoe honeymoon
confess that you watched her undress
for years before you'd met,
that you brought friends to your room
and won their admiration
by selling glimpses of her?
She is then burdened, a priest to your penitence.

And what if, like in a movie, she
had been watching you all those years,
making an object of you? Does that settle the guilt?

Or maybe she'd known all along
that you were watching.

Say she'd performed
for the eyes outside her window, turning
just as the sweater passed over her breasts.

Does she become less than an object?
Your guilt into anger.

                    ○

Part of the weight of age is living
with what we've done to our souls,
the rage that cripples
later in life.

DOWN THERE
for Karen Smythe

The marine archaeologist says,
"We have just begun
to scratch the surface."
A project that would seem as difficult
as bailing it with cheese cloth.
Raking nails across,
digging troughs that collapse
in a spitting sea.

On the ship deck he rests
his arm against the bathysphere
as if posing with his first car.

"There are temples beneath the waves," he says,
"Temples below, abandoned."

The sea hand grasping and all went down,
leaving nothing of the stones
but the infinite surface
about to be scratched.

The Most Probable Response

One morning, he heard his full name spoken aloud,
deep in his left ear, by a woman with a Chinese accent.

His mother pulled out all three names when she thought he'd
been bad,
but the voice that morning was not scolding.
The nice woman with a voice like feathers
had read his name from a clipboard or a dog-tag.

He thought about madness for a moment.
The chemicals in his brain
reflected on their relationship
to the sparks in his body.
And he chose to think of the voice as a voice—
faraway, someone who had reason to say his name,
all three of his names, a perfectly good reason.

In an office somewhere, the Bureau of Public Naming,
or at a job he'd applied for; maybe he'd been bad after all,
the woman with the voice thought.

Then, later in the day, a perfume he could not identify
made him think of a garden and clothes hanging to dry,
made him think of the summer
before it gives way to the thought of its end.

He didn't think much more of it than that.

Eastern Standard Time

At three-twenty, on a Friday in October,
a nipple appeared in the sky
above a cramped neighbourhood
in Southwestern Ontario.

It hovered several miles up, and drifted
as if sliding
down the windshield of a parked car.

A film rained everywhere,
although no clouds were visible.
The lawn became slick
and the unidentified man
holding the camera slipped.

The object is lost for a moment
then comes into view again
after a breathy search
of the sky and tree line.

There is the beat of the blue sky
scuttled with cloud.

At six-forty:
The wait to begin feels like falling.
There is always something
to prepare for, to
dread or anticipate, a longing.

I find myself about to begin,
or in motion, beginning,
never quite arriving, arrived.

Seven forty-five:
A violation to feel
yourself so watched
that, bringing the cup to your mouth,
you pretend to drink.

Like the killdeer
pretending to limp
in the gravel yard behind the house.

I felt strongly that a bird was necessary.

A Kind of Remembrance

Halfway through the first signature,
I stop, mark the page and close the book
to see the old poet, his picture
on the back cover looking younger,
more vital than my mirror in the best light.

You can chase history into myth—its edges
dulled, nothing remaining of the original
inhabitants who stepped like souls
for a time and left no wheel
or foundation—and never get tired.

My grandfather found an arrowhead
in his garden, in the stop of land that became
his garden, and brought the worked stone,
like a jagged spade from a playing card,
to the dinner table.

It may have helped
to fell a deer that fed a family.
It may have missed altogether;
lost in the woods until time covered it—
leaves, moss, the decaying forest covered it.

II

Maps to the Underworld (2)

When Orpheus goes down
the yellow dot that he is
blips from the screen, a candle
becoming a stick again,
flame into the air defused,
a note settling into memory
once the tune has played.

He leaves his car keys on the table,
his wallet on the nightstand
in the hotel room near the Gate.
His mind is on the bone gift
for the three-mouthed dog.

Let it fight itself, tear itself
blind at the post, and Orpheus—
just the shadow scent of his hand
on one tongue, fangs from both sides
snapping in—will slip by.
Mad from its own blood,
Cerberus has gone literal:
a new Ouroboros
devouring, devoured.

And maybe Dante in another reel is watching,
reading the arch for his dismissal. But here
everything is older, more dream than story.

Here is Orpheus going down without a signal,
even the sun forgets him, his author
forgets Ariadne's trick, no string
to draw him, unreflecting to light.

And when Orpheus goes down
the rest of us don't stop.
We just keep going, our lives going
with the pulse of all that is around us
going.

And when Orpheus is down
the bright movements of the sky
are still as bright
and the stars are marvelled at
just as frequently.

APPARITION

At the funeral
a woman no one has met
leaves a singed flower,

hugs the strange mourners
and vanishes
without a door,
    without mirrors.

After her kiss
I could rise,
but someone's removed my heart.

Maybe We Are Left With

Maybe we are left with
all that flesh could not signify:
the words on the tip,
the tongue defining it edge.
Vague, indecipherable,
somewhere in the belly
a quilted sorrow,
all thought and its absence.

Bees on the breath.
No, do not say Spirit.
The language is corrupt.
But to yourself say, aspire.
Soul moves the world—

runes in the field.

He leaves his glasses at home,
so he can ask for directions.

Squinting at parked cars,
he says, "Are those robots?"

"Things fall apart."

                    o

We spent three years on *the boy who fell into himself*—
know its chapters, take quotations from it
like gospel from the widening shelf.

o

This poem is inventing itself right now,
worried about time and death.

o

In Alberta and elsewhere, we eat
the continent's heart. Rip the evidence
from its soil.

o

In a flub of release
the young anchor weighs in
with the revelation that she
doesn't have a flatscreen TV at home.
The sports guy double-takes like he was taught
in J-school, and the meteorologist smiles
a suitable grin. "Death is coming," he says,
pawing at the continent behind him.

Somewhere, the quilted sorrow springs its knot
into a new disease cured by telethon,
and the bicycle farmer throws old sprockets
from a high-rise window
to decorate the lawn.

Auto/bio

My grandmother had me wear
grandfather's ring to the wake.

We were dazed shepherds,
my brothers and me.

I had watched his death
from a distance
cocooned in my own hell,
a surfeit of self.

When my father called
the night I walked through fog,
the old man briefly there,

I asked if I should come home.
"I don't know, son," he said.
He had never called me son before.

My brothers lived close to the death,
the agony and acrimony.

One brother went screaming.

I stayed the night
in grandma's apartment,
sleeping on a cot in the living room.
On guard duty I guess.

The glinting moon pulsed
from grandpa's heavy ring, a mist cube,
that she'd slammed
on the table and told me to wear.

The morning of the funeral
I chauffeured the screaming brother
in our grandfather's minivan.

Although we'd not spoken in five years,
he was full of advice and sobbed beside the corpse
like he'd expected a birthday party.

And grandma took back the ring,
gave it to my brother and said,
"Put this on your grandfather's finger."

The skin stretched like springless rubber,
the band grazing the knuckle,
and we thought she'd bury it with him.

Three days pass, and the ring again.

The weight of it these years.

The Lost and Their Noise

On the sidewalk as the hottest day
leads into a record for the coldest night,
someone picks up the familiar
sentiment—"Exactly. Exactly.
It blew my fucking mind"—that someone else
left the evening before,

and, between sidewalks, engines
amped higher than jets
fling voracious tires
to the next red light.

o

We disappear in the noise.
The television, its manifold
barkers howling the butcher's count.

We are lost and forgetful
of the time we've put in.

Anonymous Poet

There are no people in his poems
yet something clings
in the churning phrase.

Maybe a leaf's edge resembles a bat wing,
summoning a chill;
the stand-in for a nightmare.
Or the wind, throwing voices,
brags of its memory.

But you will find no people in his poems
—prepare yourself for loneliness—
and no acclaim for rockstars or presidents.
The history he pulls from is the memory of seed,
the vestigial path toward another go around.

Go, he says, find someone in your poems.

How It Happens

The procreative mind,
call it diseased. Like the time
in the Mexican restaurant
when he stared at the breasts
of the woman at the next table.
She wore a chartreuse tank top
and to top it off, just as everyone
caught him looking, he recognized her
from grade school, and remembered
how he'd cornered her at a friend's house,
some wild imbalance having taken
him, cornered the girl and not having
the heart to grab her as he'd dimly planned,
just stood there. It was the fear
in her face, like a creature at its death,
that stopped him and made him want to grab her
even more, but made him sick a little bit too.

She practiced kicking him in the groin
just as he practiced at being a rapist.
He knew she loved him somewhat
and didn't want to kick him
but wanted to just the same.

He remembered how she ran to the street
and the cool air through the open door,
the vileness in him receding,
and the friend on the couch

laughing in wonderment. It was
for the best, anyway. That house
was crazy and no place
for a young woman.

Follow That Droid

The first time I saw Star Wars, the ships blasting from the brow
toward a distant moon, the space battle
and the asthmatic knight were what caught
and held me for years, enacted in schoolyard rites.

The next time I saw Star Wars, I noticed that Princess Leia
didn't wear a bra and thanked the Force for videotape
and remote control rewind; although slow motion replay,
which would have been handy, had yet to be invented.

When I watch it now, I see all these things
and see the brief arc, my life compressed into 40 plus years;
how by the simple chance of the red droid's bad motivator,
R2 might have been left with the scrap dealer
and there'd have been no one to lead the boy to the old man.

PUNDITS

It's a job
being contrary
obstructionist
the unreasonable voice
opposing the rational measure.

It pays well:
an hour a week
for the cameras
a book deal with two commas in it,
chalkboard and foley artist
to accent gesture and expression,

a fan club.

Easily it gets under the skin—
hooked before it begins.
The power to keep minds
from changing,
the power to lock in prejudice,
to send them out with placards.

They will go, wearing turbans
and carrying pictures of the president
dressed as an organ grinder's monkey.
Nothing is too outlandish.

After the rally comes the laughter,
"Don't they know I'm joking?"

This ignorance is amber.

Dug up in a century
nothing remains of the subtle minded.
Maybe a building, a book,
a theory scrawled in dust
on the bamboo floor.

But you will find the determined
ten centuries later
still wearing their death
penalty hats, the lies they lived by
pinned to their chests,
their deflated cheeks scrying
the doom that approaches.

They wear down like stone.
The wind shaves them
away in layers and the clouds they form
block the sun for generations.

o

Let me always return
to the air as vapour not as dust,
the prayer of the subtle mind.

Let Us Now Invent the Past

There was that time
in someone's childhood
when bad things didn't happen.
Young people became old people.
A graduate found a job
and defined a life.
Parents honoured children,
although it wasn't called for.
And a teacher's hand
on the back of his student
was a comfort, not a reason
to call the lawyers.

Its innocence derived from nostalgia,
as much as ignorance of Greek tragedy,
that perfect age we came from
is peopled with harmless eccentrics:
The first man in town to own hip waders;
The three-legged dog
drinking milk from doorstep bottles;
The nun who went mad
trying to kiss her own lips;
And the big man stacking lumber
for the space program
while the Woman-So-Beautiful-
She-Became-Your-Mother watched
laughing, her teeth compared to pearls

by a poet who wrote a column
in the local paper.

It's not a bad place, this past no one had,
this place that returns to us
in the burn of time on flesh.

The Analysis

There is no denying the blood.
Its count laid out in parts and numbers,
the disease extrapolated by ratio.
I was expecting death and a lecture
on diet and medication.
The prescription pad, like an order form
near the pharmaceutical catalogue
on the counter by the bottle of tongue
depressors, and the pen on top of it,
almost filling itself in.

"I think the benefits outweigh the risks,"
she says. I would be more confident
if she wore a stethoscope now and then.

o

Read the blood, a table of contents
to this burning book. The only deficit, as far
as I can tell, a chronic lack of cannabinoids.

Everything else is abnormally high.

Found Missing

In Hammurabi's rulebook, which he took down
from the sun in some versions, from a lesser star
in others, there was nothing written
about love and turning cheeks, it was all
eye for eye, a life for an accusation.

From it, witch-hunters inherited the water test.
The river as judge decided with its currents
whether the accused did it or not. If not,
the accuser was given his death. If so,
the accuser inherited the drowned man's goods.

Not a bad deal, all said. Either way, there was one
fewer mouth to feed. But it certainly
made one want to practice at swimming, to
become lighter than water. There were only
strong swimmers in Babylon. And the drowned.

The difference between Hammurabi and, say, Joseph Smith
is mostly that we can see tablets in their original
form, whereas the gold leaf Smith read from disappeared
with Maroni or whomever the thin stranger
who visited was, leaving only Smith's translation.

The same thing, really. Because no one, as far as
I can tell, saw the sun god handoff
to Hammurabi, no one but Hammurabi himself,
and you can never trust a king to tell the truth
about what's going on. Everything is mythic to a king.

Millennia, chopped away like hands, falling
and rising in dust, covering the cities, have erased
the knowledge of flight, of distant talk. It will take
all that time again to regain the faintest
efficiencies. And look how far we've come.

A short time of centuries, and we have gained back
incandescence and the poisoning of wells
through sewer veins, but in a larger well, a more invasive
incandescence; the entire ocean a well, Gehenna spilled over
every inch that humans touch. I have seen it.

A short time of centuries, and we gaze ourselves blind
watching ourselves reflected, our selves entranced
by the vision we had of our selves, in chains
yet unbound, chained to the toxic history we have
invented and follow as if on rails. Mercy.

Half a mina for a tree poached from your neighbour's land.
The same price for a blow that takes a woman's life.
Or, if the woman loses a child from his strike,
his daughter is put to death. Hammurabi doesn't say
what the man without a daughter loses. A whole mina?

One mina is sixty shekels, or thirteen bucks, my computer
tells me. Hammurabi's gold standard, a life for six and one-
half dollars, which can't buy your way out of a taxi cab
these days, won't put you in a movie seat. But I complain
of things that no longer matter. We are deserted.

By our histories, deserted. Beginnings with no ending.
Beginning to begin, to begin at the middle of things,
much as a dream begins by being. We are, and to remind us,
we tear the chain roots from the ground, our pasts
dissolving in the steady light, Times Square. Indefinite.

If I promised Hammurabi I would not steal the prized vase
from the Museum of Inequities and really meant at that moment
"I will not steal," but find in a different moment a need
to steal the vase—I don't know, maybe your life depends on it—
and steal the vase, did I lie?

And is it worth lying to Hammurabi to have the vase
for a spittoon at the bar, to marvel at in private, and fawn
at the lithe gods in honeycomb beards who dance in tableau
a Sumerian rite that Hammurabi himself has forgotten? Braggarts
might swoon at the prize, but I count the parts I will lose when it's found missing.

For this theft chained to a rock overlooking the vacuous sea.
A nice view for those few moments on waking, the blind pain
of the night before cooled by the morning, watching the dark
squiggle from the horizon grow into a raven, and before the first
tuck of its beak into the belly, a simple kind of bliss.

But that is not Hammurabi's solution. For him it's the hand
that must be excised, as if the hand had offended on its own.
In a small cell, the severed hands of thieves plot escape. Wait
until the guard has fallen into his hash slumber, pick the lock
with curved nails, then scale the harsh brick to the ground.

On their own, the hands are blind, groping through the grass
for a familiar texture. Maybe a set of eyes plucked out
or a pair of feet removed for kicking a free man can be found
and befriended. Maybe a wanderer with a stump wrist will stop,
recognizing the knot of veins or the curve of a fingernail.

Were there prosthetic limbs in Babylon? Finely geared mechanisms
like clocks, banded with pulleys and alive with sprockets, digits carved
from pomegranate and lashed to the wrist with leather straps
and suction cups, designed by the son or brother of the hatchet man.
They share office space in the same squat hut. Was this Babylon?

Looking back on the things we look back upon, Babylon wondered
at its origins, as much placed there then as we are placed here now, as lost
and rootless in time, as decentred by the certainty of the dust
we become. The flood before the reclamation of humanity, the voice
of the old man who remembers it all, and the mountain we have not yet climbed.

It was never, it was always, it was always never that we
struggled to name our selves in the torrential rumble of things
around us. The world was not always silent. There were rivers
louder than anything. And the forests creaking with our fears,
the sound of the sky echoing at night, gliding our minds to the stars.

If the water takes her, she was innocent. This is European fatalism.
Too bad, too late. To Hammurabi, the spirit of water preserved the innocent,
drowning the adulteress. It is no surprise that miraculous conceptions
are uncountable in stories from the time. What priest of the court proclaimed
the miracle of the Queen's pregnancy? Her son a king, the embodiment of the
impregnating god.

Horus, Krishna, Zarathustra, Noah, Pythagoras, Plato, Alexander, Mithras, Buddha, John, Jesus, born out of mysterious unions more mysterious than the mystery of coitus. We were told of Jesus' virginal birth before we were told about sex. All we needed to know was an unnamed sin brought us into being and Jesus was free of that sin. So was Dolly, the cloned ewe.

On to that vase, its mouth like the rim of a bubble that popped and froze, drying in the treeless desert, into a ring that lets the broad belly commune with the broader air, too cracked to hold anything but leaves and bones, too uneven the cracks to measure the flow of sand; still, a watering jug it might make for dry, distant gardens.

Keats found a beauty I do not find. My stolen vase collects dirty socks in the corner of the basement apartment where I dreamed of sacrificing my virginity to the greater cause. For he so loved the world that he gave his purity to know the sin everyone was talking about, and found it to be highly overrated, addictive, and difficult to engineer.

But that vase, its battle scenery, a melange of swords and horses, bright daggers from the brow of an extinct god mowing through the unidentified enemy as if it had been made of air, of pure story, just the breath of fearful seers, and the unutterable markings, as if a water bird drunk on fermented swamp root had rolled it like a log while the clay was still wet.

Silent. The laws needn't speak anymore, the edge and line of each character tattooed on our character, assumed as good manners, justice, housed in courts wherever there is history. The sun, now aware of its radius, is no longer fixed on Earth, no longer watching the shadows we make. The sun is not interested in our shadows.

45

How to Move On

Leg trapped? Lose it.
Crawl if you have to,
just move.
Even if you are still
you can move, so move.

When I rut in past disappointments,
someone from the balcony shouts:
"Don't dwell. Keep it moving."
And I think of the walls where I've dwelled,
the ideas on shelves,
in frames, that kept me
comforted, confined.
And of *dwell* itself,
how we arrived at *home*,
dwelling, from *dwellan*,
"to deceive, to go astray."

For those of us who know the road,
home is a brief distraction,
a going-astray from the true state of things,
a bubble maybe, the illusion of permanence.

But let us not dwell on it.

Stopped rivers stagnate.
Although it is peopled by campers

and water skiers, it is
no lake.

I had luck in this spot once,
standing against the warm brick,
the air thick as a lake, under the parking lot neon.
And I wrote about a bicycle
about to be stolen.

And watched as you stared
into the crumbling distance

just as my pen ran out.

III

Maps to the Underworld (3)

Orpheus was hard to live with when he got back to ground.

Crawling from the Earth, a poet.

There were the birds with membranous wings
in the trees that crackle with night winds.

And there were the rough toads, their songs
from the pond grass, their eyes everywhere.

Nowhere. He remembers crawling and little more.
He remembers counting the fistfuls of dirt
that he clutched away revealing
the sky he could never quite reach.

Mortal Misprision

I think to die last is worse;
leaving first, we avoid our deaths,
the tattooed reminder grief makes.

The body I am building has few scars.
There is nothing that clings to skin
so far
and walking—
  deserts, highways, forests, paths—
keeps the inevitable chill at bay.
But it will come. Eventually
we see the skull face in the street,
looking in at candle-lit windows.

The weatherman in a suitable grin says,
"Death is coming."

But I'm never sure.
The night before, another voice
said, "Pathless beginnings,"
although that's not what it said,

and yesterday, the library
was the best escape route.

o

Atonement means we find

no revulsion in the other
and looking, we see no other—
just the whole self dreaming.

I knew god had found me
when I fell in love
with the barista's brown wart
and he with my stutter.

WAR

We have come to this before
and know its end already:
    to end all
and continue on the same way
    to a war
and back, home and broken.

The dead are poured to their graves
as the next platoon yowls from the womb.

For once, can the man on the corner
be right about Judgement?

We take evening tea at the defendant's table,
the bought jury adding up our days and torture
before the closing arguments.

NYC

The towers have us now,
our necks pensive
bows charged with arrows,
we aim our eyes
to this or that;
the window open
and the street
outside coming in.

When you're not watching,
history (avoid it) snaps
down an imprint
welded from iron rods and
linked in rude knots
carried by barge
across the slow river.
In winter, dragged
on skis, the pure weight
helping the skid.

The city is like this:
open and troubled
at the singed edge,
a flower one time
aflame, now silent
in the cool afterdeath.
An unscripted buoyancy,
the witch floats

away to a movie deal
and lunchbox portraits,
syndicated columns on
hair dye and broomstick
maintenance. I am wondering
where did the witch
come from in all this?
Where does she live now
that newspapers
have folded and bundled
themselves for burning?

Hitler signs for a taxicab
at 4th and 45th,
surgical gloves mounded
around his feet.
Does anyone notice the stranger
bending coloured bars after rain,
hanging a test pattern horseshoe
over our heads?

Where there were none, it seems
people have returned to relearn
and nudge
the ship from its current.

We are too easily there,
assumed to be
there even when we're not,
so never mind for now

the people in pants and shirts,
dresses or skirts, swinging
twin-handled bags and boasting
of their prey, unnoticing the river
that is riding them.

I am reading the book
of the McGraw Rotunda,
the ornate binding, its words
milling around
behind camera flashes.

I would like to live
in a city where the public
library is a tourist attraction.

In its box, a Gutenberg,
one of a dozen or so.

The lady in short-distance shoes
sees me looking,
looks back to see
what I'm looking at
although familiarity has made her
blind, the entire wonder—
the unmatched structure,
built by Keynes' restless shovel
and never again on this earth,
now declining—as common to her
as the sun.

Dredging

Because it is claimed the river has fallen,
a floating backhoe and an empty barge
anchor where the channel divides.

One day I will understand the river:
dark, ruffled, described in two ways.
And the pale sky, I'll understand it too.

A voice (mine, most likely) says
it won't be long before I move
from this disgruntled paradise
to someplace that is
possibly no place.
The gate tips away to make
a bridge across the moat
and not long from now
the thing that I am will leave.
I'm sure of it, feel it more soundly
than I've felt anything untouchable.
It may be years or next week,
fifty years perhaps but it will come—
an unknown elsewhere, a farflung sea.
I was just passing
through and knew it all along.
Much of the time
was grace to be wasted
on tv and masturbation,
jobs that paid squat

but ate time
and that's all right;
that time was for wasting.
But now it's the fine lens that sees,
now the open eye recalls,
now the loss is recovered
and there are ghosts all around.

Take in the page,
one glance.
Is the word
masturbation
all that stands
out, as if
on a line all its own?

If so, you
may have been perverted
as the old song goes,
and I don't know
what to do about that
but to say
I am not responsible
for your bicycle
if you leave it
unlocked beside me.
Who knows how long
I will be here?

New America

Watching now, in the age of the perfected image,
the early television performer,
eyes lined in black marker,
flapjack-faced and sweating,
is wholly unreal.
Was everyone in the 50s greasy
or just the people on TV? I ask
because no one looks like that today:
flat and greasy, sopping sweat
under the rude lights.

What I saw was different from what
you see now and somehow about the same.
The dreamed enactments
sponsored by dish soap
and flavoured tobacco
tell only the ideal and its opposite;
as in a mirror, it is
reflexive of someone else.
Leave her alone! The house wife
is fine with the shape her waist takes on.
She does not need another voice
in her living room shouting
about her dull floors and the grime
around her husband's collar,
nor does she need a pious news anchor
blasting the world for its violence
to bring the jihad home.

Across the lawn the flag
will never reach top-staff.
Cut the tips from the flagpoles.
We will mourn the death
of our ideation; the streets
too crowded for processionals,
we march with stump legs,
no legs at all, past dream shops
and boutiques that deal in Bryce Canyon replicas
made from sugar grown on slave islands.
How much for that new washer with
double agitator, and how can we get it for less?

LITTLE THINGS

So what if you can't smoke pot,
you can't eat it or wear it in most places either.
Too gentle of a thing, too easily renewed.
Vandana Shiva called it a "devious mind"
that would break the cycle of the seed.

And I write a lot about seeds
knowing little about them really
but always default to seed
this and seed that
like I expect something to grow
from these pages.

UNSPOKEN

There is something I need to say
and will say
once the omelette's made.

Steam in fine wisps from the warming pan.
Eggshells are fragile until you want them broken.
Then they split into shards only the shell
can scoop up. Two orange yolks
float in the common white,
separate for a time then whisked
into the same bland lather.

I need to say something that has
nothing to do with love.
Love does not need saying.

Mushroom slices shrink under heat,
get darker, softer
like things kept from rain too long,
things gone dry in shelter.

But the hissing pan
is the only sound from the kitchen.
There is something I need to say.

White cheddar dissolves
unseen except where the edges
harden and brown.

There is something about eggs
and feet gone numb from years
walking the same path.

But to say it would ruin our meal,
bring a long blathering that we
will never fully resolve.

THE SCREEN BEHIND THE CURTAIN

In today's science journal:
the bones of a giant rat,
forty times larger than the ones
we know, were dug
from antediluvian depth.

As children we knew everything
had been bigger once, more lyrical:
Rapacious mosquitoes humming thunder
chased us through primordial playgrounds.
Cats, too, were larger. And not that long ago.

As with cats, so with poets.

I imagine the bones of Walt Whitman
cramped in his crypt.
And Emily Dickinson's bewildering skull,
the cabinet where her ghosts were kept,
gazing eyeless from a posthumous shelf.

It's said we are taller by a foot
than even a century ago.
It's the food, too much of it,
and easy lives that spring us
weightless into the air.

This might be true.

I have sat in thimble seats
in old movie houses
waiting for curtains
to part or rise.

Cocoons Like Cabin Doors

I

Before the drought, we ached for resolution
to the body's transformations.

Stumbling, near-aquatic mass one moment,
edged and toothy soon after.

On the eve of miracles,
one long night hanging above us

and the next necessary
movement of wing about to happen,

how could I have been here
and no place at once?

Our private Utopia was shattered
by a rising brow,

doubt
destroyed it.

On certain days, I have struggled
to stay between the lines.

II

As children we perched
on the front step,

too frightened to enter
the night, and held our bodies

above the ground,
swinging out with the door,

bending the door-hinge
with our rhyming games,

waiting for dawn's orange light
and the fall from dreamed-up grace.

III

Seeing the world made of lines,
the porch carpet, a vast abyss

blurring under our feet,
and close to that, the lines

of horizon, shades and folds,
the panoptic day approaching,

I knew I could leap down
and up again and change

everything; even lines beyond the abyss,
splash into being when I jump like that.

It is, you said, perception
that awakens us.

All this time, I thought
it was the butterfly.

New Clothes

It'll be just like the Swiss Family Robinson, only with more cursing!
We're gonna live like kings! Damn, hell, ass kings! —Bart Simpson

Oh, we're going to live.
We will effing G.D. live
all right, but it's going to hurt
like a pine tree rooted in the heart.
The slow sap routing through veins,
tearing at the lines and joints
of the frames we put around
the things we've loved.

I knew you when you were the tree
I dreamed of climbing
but was not allowed to climb.
Not because I might fall,
although that was the fear implanted,
the mechanism of dissuasion,
but because of the stains
left on pants and shirts,
the bits of bark that cling to fabric,
the moss bleeding green.

There were two types of children
in the cool haze after summer storms.
Some in their new boots
avoided puddles and plucked grass blades
from their yellow shanks.

And some ran spastic through the pond,
stood in the deepest parts,
the water mounting the lips
of their folded boot tops.

And a third type I'd forgotten about
until now
who navigated the pond, stepping
from rock to log, and sometimes fell.

IV

Fancy Clapping

What is the story of our heads.
Who is the movement of bodies.

An evening of sitting brings us
to the moment when the juggler

incites the room into clapping
the steady, marching beat of one

two, three, four while he runs a tight
circle under levitating

torches that never seem to drop
close enough to his hand to be

thrown up into the air again.
Is he even necessary?

The miracle seems self-contained.
By itself a thing to behold.

The juggler is just in the way
and has no claim on perception.

Next to me a woman who smells
gently of vomit cannot catch

the rhythm of one, two, three, four
and throws the whole row off by two

beats that we never recover.
There is a hesitation in her

as if an invisible spring
hovers between her hands, as if

her palms were charged with opposing
currents and repel each other

for just the blip of a second,
long enough to make an echo

that adds up to an extra beat
and throws the juggler off his game.

Arrhythmia spreads
along our row and jumps the aisle.

It moves like a wave through the crowd
until everyone begins to doubt

the rhythm they've carried.
The juggler's assistant comes on stage,

clapping hands like a country song
and the whole room follows again.

That's when someone I cannot see
decides to emphasize a beat.

He or she makes a tent of two
like the point of an EKG

that goes flat after a brief spike.
The accent is a crease that folds

the marching applause on itself,
and reminds me of the trouble

that accents give in translation:
oh YA or OH ya—be cautious.

Finally smoothed to the flat four,
the rhythm builds up a volume

so the canned music can't be heard
and hooting from the balcony

is drowned completely in a square
din that sounds like boots trudging home.

That is when a gang of drummers
arriving after a late gig

introduce angles to the square.
Fit five into four, nine into eight.

They play against the room, lay counterpoint
across the steady flash, fancy clapping the juggler

into orbit. He drops the baton to the stage and runs
to the back of the theatre. The fire hose he thought

he'd seen before the show is nowhere. He runs
farther, through the exit, with the audience inside

fancy clapping itself to ash.

Cedar Grove

On lockdown at lunchtime
and on the ward's door a sign
asking visitors to keep everything closed.

I see her through the window
adjusting her napkin
sitting with three others at the square table.
She might know them,
they could have been friends in sprightly times.
They may have quarrelled over boys,
argued about the correct way to raise children,
shared recipes at neighbourhood picnics—
leaving out one part to ensure immortality.

Sitting now with all that forgotten,
remembering only where food goes in,
nothing is as they'd dreamed
in this dim afterlife, lived while still alive.

A woman has been howling for twenty minutes,
the whole time that I've waited for lunch to end.
Between breaths, she chants, "Kill me, Jesus."

No one is listening. She's become another sound,
like the piped-in music, like the John Wayne movie
that is always on. Is that where Grandmother is going?
A senseless cry, unanswered, unanswerable?

Is that where we go should we live?

He

The first decades chasing hips,
wanting, debauching.

The middle years defending
his imagined daughters
from younger versions of himself.

The last years recognizing
his powerlessness to do either.

Resurrection by Garden Trowel

A poem should not limit or filter influence but acknowledge.
—from *A Poem Should*, author unknown

I have protected these poems from glenn beck and paris hilton,
barack obama, and george w. bush, and from stephen harper
and elizabeth may, david suzuki, and most everyone
(but you

for you
these poems never close, the kettle waits.
I have turned down the sheets;
if you get tired of reading
you can rest upstairs with the meter and the rhyme).

I let bowering into a poem once
and he made a mess of the place
shot the lights out, dug the dog
up from the garden.

The room he stayed in
is stripped to the frame
revealing the cage we build our houses around.

lady gaga, topless on oprah, and oprah, always
in clothing, cannot buy their way into these poems.

And what this poem does, no one will notice.

A Fragment

You have been plying sounds and voices
into pictures drawn in words;

and that is one way to go.

What
who
and where

is the trouble
with answers.

After some puttering,
at last the image:
the serpent cat
rising from low muck.

Is a lake
drained of water
still a lake?

And around it the thin machine's
sharp approach, the razzed senses.
Ratting for its stone brood,

the serpent cat calls in long prayers
as the fire wheel rips the clouds
and lightning holds up the sky.

The new hydra has come
for the serpent cat's blood,
everything else has gone dry.

It rises from the other place,
tastes its fangs. Its tongue
is eyed and watching.

In the dreamed life, a possible future,
the lake is collared with a dam
and the serpent cat stretches its back against a shield
half milled-out, chipped away but rising on the hydra.

Until the humans are gone
back into dust,
only the breath against the machine.
Its slow heel
deep in the soil,
deep on the rock,
in the earth and ocean.

Hydra, its circuits ebullient,
each part of it recombining:
toasters flung from breakfast tables

call through shadows
thinking of the lives we become
in becoming ourselves for the day.

Too Hot for Monkey

August cats plod lonely.
Their fur sticks to the hand like gum.
If she could ask one question
it might be why I call her Monkey
when her name is Loo.
It's confusing to have so many
names to ignore.

One day, I tell her,
I will catch you distracted
and stumble across the name
that reels you to me.

Until then I call from a roulette
wheel of names, just glad that we are
aware of each other
briefly while the planet's afire,
and grateful that our bowls are full.

Too Quick for Art

A secret in muscle
exposed with a sudden movement.
Near the end, change is too quick for art,
just revolution without reflection.

A secret in the muscle reveals the poacher's trophy.
Impulse is an argument for dominance.
Humans wear the skins of their rivals
and change the ecology by removing the farmer.

Volts and wages escalated into industrial crises:
the crisis of municipalities and rail lines,
cobbled roads and pine-choked districts
stripped of pine.

The Unforeseen

Before I knew anything, a neighbour
who'd lost half a finger
to the butcher's block,
said, "The things you don't figure
are what bind you to ground."

He'd put his knuckle to his nostril
and you'd swear he had the whole thing
up his nose until he showed you
where the round blade had made meat of him.

All the things that bind you to ground
are blessings. Flight was never promised.
The equation has its own balance.
Alter it, but nothing will change
until the day it does.

INTERFERENCE

After the rain, the city shakes itself
dry in the chill night.

Drivers moan their steady wheels
down streets, the same as in heat.

Young men, uncertain of their tongues,
scatter fuck into what's left of quiet,

and just as a thought opens its green arms
to the image of a dreamed-up sun,

a street washer closes the air,
scrubbing everything from the mind.

A friend said the universe is perverse,
explaining how someone will walk

into the room just when we get to the work
we've been kept from. It contrives

to keep us from completion.
It prolongs the game awhile.

A Short Round

Oops

When his voice bored him
he stopped talking.

He noticed the waitress
listening then.

And other people,
he noticed them too.

The baker's thumb,
painted like an Easter egg.

He saw his mother,
the lines he'd etched
around her eyes, the years
he'd shot out of her.

When his voice finally bored him,
he heard the wind
he thought he could ignore,
its growl and the windows
it pawed.

So much had happened,
he couldn't keep track.
There was the brother he'd lost
somewhere and the angels
in duncecaps hallooing the sun,
every morning.

There was so much,
a history to bear.

Give me a god who says:
It is the same heaven.
You've seen it—
here, try again.

First Poem

It was a poem of accusation,
of unrequited invitations,
of jealousy of song.

Some pearl-voiced singer
sang to everyone around
but not specifically to her
and she wanted a song
to contain her, although she knew
no song could.

She read, having never spoken before,
scratching her ankle
through the cuff of her jeans
scratching a vaudeville rhythm.
There were words
and the scratching, my mind
couldn't hold both,
and the ant or vague insect
that crawled out of her leg.
It stitched across the painted floor,

coming like a cat
to a person afraid of cats.

I moved my foot away
and it made up the new distance,
all six or eight of its legs

swallowed the space,
and I knew I'd end up crushing it,
which I did
but with some reservation—just
a tap of the sole against the cement floor,
painted a soupy red anyway
like watery blood.

The ant writhed and shivered
and I watched it die
not certain what it was that I'd killed.

THE JOKE

The joke gets tired, okay?
That's the first thing you should know
about humour and why the joke
after ten years
lay down in the street
to wait for a car
to take memory away.

It's not as if I have nothing else to do.
There are the blades of grass
that need polishing and the pine cones
that no one has volunteered to count.

The world doesn't just invent itself:
it needs some coaching, a poke
to remind it that invention
has always been necessary.

And there are more subtle necessities,
like jellyfish and unicorns.
Things the earth could not
think up on its own and so
thought us up.

Without our divine concession,
the deal we made with the thing called god
that brought us here, awake, in the first place,

there'd be nothing.

It is easy to forget all that we've made.
We've left much of it stranded
as we made for dry ground.
The book we were excited about
until someone told us it wasn't really that good,
kind of a bad book in fact.
The writer must have known someone,
or paid to have it published.
Who else would go through all that trouble over nothing?

The serious heat of summer
is what I remember most of the invention,
days when the joke went on and on.

Notes and Acknowledgements

The early drafts of these poems were written from May to September, 2010. A fair number stem from a short trip to New York City that summer. The rest were written on the waterfront in Sault Ste. Marie, Ontario. The manuscript underwent many revisions during the winter of 2010/11. More revisions, additions and extractions were made through the summer and fall of 2011, with another full revision in December, 2011. This slow process of development was helped along by some fine editorial advice from Karen Smythe. Further thanks in the editorial department are sent to Laurence Steven for his close and careful reading of the material. Thanks too to Jesus Hardwell for giving it a read.

I wish to thank poet Gary Barwin for the marvellous clapping dog-head image on the front cover and for his generous support.

To Lorna Crozier and Patrick Lane, who, through their work and kindness, have mentored and encouraged a generation of Canadian poets: thank you.

I am grateful to Tobias Wolff whose memoir *This Boy's Life* was a good companion during the early stages of this book.

The staff, management, faculty and (most of all) students at Sault College form the supportive community essential for collective education. I am privileged to continue my education within that community. Thank you.

Thanks to Laurence and Jan Steven and all at Scrivener Press.

Once again I wish to acknowledge the Ontario Arts Council and the editors who participate in the Writers' Reserve Grant program.

Mostly, I thank Maria for sharing this surreal existence.

Poet and songwriter Mark D. Dunn lives in Sault Ste. Marie, Ontario and teaches at Sault College. *Fancy Clapping* is his second collection of poetry. Dunn's poems have won the Ted Plantos Memorial Award. His previous collection, *Ghost Music*, was longlisted for the 2011 Relit Awards. He can be found on the web at www.mddunn.com